CW00337148

How to Become

THE

MAN

The Myth

THE

LEGEND

CHARISMA · BRAVERY · FITNESS · HUMOUR

BE THE MAN, THE MYTH, THE LEGEND

An exclusive edition for

This edition first published in Great Britain in 2018 by Allsorted Ltd, Watford, Herts, UK WD19 4BG

© Susanna Geoghegan Gift Publishing

Author: Roffy
Cover design: Milestone Creative
Contents design: Double Fish Design Ltd

ISBN: 978-1-911517-40-5

Printed in China

LEGEND OR LOSER?

So, what does it take to

★ BE A LEGEND ★

Definitions vary.

Some believe that it takes years of hard work and dedication to become the very best in their field. Others consider a legend to be a selfless, compassionate and charismatic leader of men.

Barry from the pub thinks a legend is someone who can down 15 lagers, list every goal scorer of the 2006 World Cup and then sing a medley of Nickelback songs in Klingon. All before his first pee of the evening.

However, Barry does all those things himself. Every Friday. And no one else considers Barry to be a legend.

Whatever your personal definition, if you want to be a legend yourself, try following in the footsteps of others that have gone before. To get you started, we've sought out the masters of sport, science, entertainment and everything in between to discover their secrets – some of them are well-known legends, others are unsung heroes.

Along the way you'll also learn the difference between a loser and a legend, discover some top tips and jokes, and, most importantly of all, find out what makes the perfect barbecue.

Don't be Barry. Be *The Man, The Myth, The Legend*.

Not Fit For
★ PURPOSE ★

A balanced workout is a key part of a legend's fitness regime. Here's how to tell if it's not working out.

Your workout consists of 15 mins of cardio, 10 mins on the defibrillator, and then 3 days in the hospital.

There's only one machine that you use at the gym and it contains chocolate bars, nuts and fizzy drinks. And you still have to wipe it down after you use it.

You think that a spin class will teach you about laundry.

You go to the gym so rarely that you still call it the James.

Your workout is mainly sit-ups because it involves the most lying down.

You think that resistance training means refusing to go to the gym in the first place.

The toughest part of your workout is putting your jeans back on while still wet from the shower.

Your workout playlist is only one song long.

MEET THE LEGEND

Muhammad
ALI

Best known as: Arguably the greatest ever boxer, winning 37 of his 61 fights by knockout.

Did you know? He became a boxer because someone stole his bike when he was 12. He reported the theft to police officer Joe Martin, vowing to pummel the culprit. Martin, also a boxing trainer, suggested he first learn how to fight. Six weeks later, he won his first bout in a split decision.

Legendary fact: Not only did Ali win the 'The Rumble in the Jungle' against George Foreman, he started the fight at 4am in the morning so it could be broadcast live on US primetime TV.

Quotable: 'I am the greatest, I said that even before I knew I was.'

LEGEND OR LOSER?

The

★ BARBECUE ★

Barbecues are great social occasions. They offer a chance to let your hair down and enjoy a bite to eat in the great outdoors. But when you are invited to dine al fresco, are you 'the man' or 'that guy'?

· CATERING FURNISHMENT ·

Legend: Brings some wine and/or beer, and a homemade salad or dessert.

Loser: Brings themselves. And possibly a six-pack of own-brand lager that they never share.

· SOCIAL INTEGRATION ·

Legend: Chats with old friends, makes some new ones.

Loser: Stares intently at the flames the entire time, never saying a word. Until the lager kicks in, then they stare intently at the prettiest guest the entire time, never saying a word.

· COMBUSTION FACILITATION ·

Legend: Lets the host get on with it. Fully prepared to find a bucket of water if required.

Loser: Throws a packet of firelighters onto the hot coals, shouting 'I am the firestarter!'

· CULINARY ASSISTANCE ·

Legend: Will always lend a hand if asked. Is not scared to chop vegetables.

Loser: Grabs the nearest spatula to flip a still-raw burger. It lands in the paddling pool. In the neighbours' garden.

· COMESTIBLE DISTRIBUTION ·

Legend: Takes a few viands from the grill, a bread roll and selection of sides. Compliments the chef on each item.

Loser: Grabs seven steaks, covers them in an entire bottle of hot sauce and eats the lot by hand.

Legends of
★ RECORD ★

So, how do you prove you're a legend to everyone?
Try breaking a World Record. Here are a few you
might want to have a crack at during your lunchbreak.

· HOT BITE ·

Russel Todd ate 70g of Carolina Reaper Chillies - one
of the hottest chillies on earth - in one minute in April
2015. His visit to the toilet the following day was also
record breaking.

· ONE FOR THE ROAD ·

Angus Wood and Ed Dupuy poured a 2,082 litre
glass of ale in July 2014. Bet I could have drunk it
in 30 seconds...

· BIG CLICKER ·

Suraj and Rajesh Kumar built a 4.5 metre long fully-
functional TV remote control in September 2015.
However, it meant that their 28' TV had to be more
than 4.5 metres away to operate it.

· IN A SPIN ·

Bernie Boehm spun a basketball on his finger for
33.25 seconds in August 2013. Doesn't sound like
much? He did it while surfing.

'THERE'S ONLY ONE THING WORSE THAN AN ESTATE AGENT, BUT AT LEAST THAT CAN BE SAFELY LANCED, DRAINED AND SURGICALLY DRESSED.'

· STEPHEN FRY ·

MAN OF MIRTH

Taller
★ TALES ★

Three cowboys from different parts of the world were sitting around a campfire, talking about how tough they were. Their tales kept getting taller and taller.

The cowboy from Australia said,
'OK you drongos, I wrestled a 200-pound crocodile and made it cry like a baby.'

The cowboy from Mexico shook his head and said, 'That's
nothing, I killed a 400-pound steer with my
bare hands.'

The cowboy from Texas just smiled and kept stirring the
campfire with his leg.

Pennies from ★ HEAVEN ★

Some legends never die. In fact, some keep raking in the big bucks after their death. According to Forbes, here are the biggest earners from 2016 who didn't let a small thing like dying get in the way.

1. MICHAEL JACKSON, $825 MILLION*

2. CHARLES SCHULZ, $48 MILLION

3. ARNOLD PALMER, $40 MILLION

4. ELVIS PRESLEY, $27 MILLION

5. PRINCE, $25 MILLION

6. BOB MARLEY, $21 MILLION

7. THEODOR 'DR SEUSS' GEISEL, $20 MILLION

8. JOHN LENNON, $12 MILLION

9. ALBERT EINSTEIN, $11.5 MILLION

10. DAVID BOWIE, $10.5 MILLION

*$750 million came from the sale of Jackson's 50% share of the Sony/ATV catalogue. Jacko normally only pulls in around $100 million a year. $100 million!!

'I THINK IT'S FASCINATING THAT I RECEIVE ATTENTION FOR WHAT PEOPLE PERCEIVE TO BE A LEVEL OF **MANLINESS OR MACHISMO,** WHEN AMONGST MY FAMILY OF FARMERS AND PARAMEDICS AND REGULAR AMERICANS, I'M KIND OF THE **SISSY IN MY FAMILY.'**

· NICK OFFERMAN ·

MEET THE LEGEND

Neil

ARMSTRONG

Best known as: The first man on the Moon.

Did you know? As a young man, he worked many odd jobs to pay for flying lessons. At one time, he earned $1 by mowing the grass in his local cemetery.

Legendary fact: Neil earned three medals for his 78 missions during the Korean war. Once on a dawn combat patrol, he saw rows and rows of North Korean soldiers, unarmed, doing their daily calisthenics. He could have mowed them down but chose to fly on. He said, 'It looked like they were having a rough enough time doing their morning exercises.'

Quotable: 'The one thing I regret was that my work required an enormous amount of my time, and a lot of travel.'

LEGEND OR LOSER?

Four

★ WHEELS ★

Whether you love the open road or just need a vehicle to get from A to B, your car says a lot about you. So, are you a demon or a duffer behind the wheel?

· ENTERTAINMENT ·

Legend: A kicking playlist from your favourite streaming service.

Loser: Cassette of nursery rhymes that was stuck in the player when you bought the car.

· TECHNOLOGY ·

Legend: Satnav, Bluetooth and in-car wifi.

Loser: 15-year-old dumb-phone duct-taped to the dashboard. 'Snake' is not a satnav.

· SAFETY ·

Legend: Passenger airbags, distance monitor and parking sensors.

Loser: A whoopee cushion taped to the steering wheel, amplifying the horn because the brakes fail so often, getting too drunk to drive.

· INTERNAL DECORATION ·

Legend: A photo of a loved one hidden behind the sun visor.

Loser: A broken hula girl and a footwell full of orange peel, parking tickets and bacon rind.

· EXTERNAL DECORATION ·

Legend: None.

Loser: Blue lights under the car because it's cool to look possessed by an evil spirit. Tinted windows because the driver wants to look like a politician or a pimp or both. Novelty stickers, a teddy bear on the front grill, headlight lashes, antlers on the hood, personalised plates, doll's head on the radio aerial, 'dick head' scratched on the passenger door by an ex ...

MAN of MIRTH

Family

★ TREE ★

Three retired soldiers, Fred, Bert and Alf, were boasting about their family's military history.

Fred said, proudly, 'My great grandfather was the youngest in his battalion at the Crimea.'

Bert countered, 'My great grandfather had a medal pinned on him by the King himself.'

Alf pondered these achievements for a moment, then said 'I tell you this. I'm the only soldier in my family, but if my great grandfather was alive today, he would be the most famous man in the world.'

'What? Why!?' puzzled Fred and Bert.

'Well,' continued Alf, 'He'd be at least 170 years old.'

'PEOPLE THINK IT MUST BE FUN TO BE A SUPER GENIUS, BUT THEY DON'T REALIZE HOW HARD IT IS TO PUT UP WITH ALL THE IDIOTS IN THE WORLD.'

· BILL WATTERSON ·

MEET THE LEGEND
Alexander von HUMBOLDT

Best known as: An explorer and founder of modern geography, described by Darwin as 'the greatest scientific traveller who ever lived'.

Did you know? He mapped 1,700 miles worth of flora and fauna in Latin America over five years on one of the most dangerous scientific expeditions ever. During his journey, he discovered that altitude mountain sickness was brought on by a lack of oxygen.

Legendary fact: He was a pioneer of climate science. Von Humboldt not only predicted man-made climate change, but, more importantly for wine lovers, he calculated the best climate conditions for growing vines.

Quotable: 'There are three stages of scientific discovery: first people deny it is true; then they deny it is important; finally they credit the wrong person.'

MAN OF MIRTH

Taming the

BEAST

Lloyd arrived at the circus and told the ringmaster that he was applying for a job as a lion tamer. The ringmaster asked if he had any experience. Lloyd said, 'Why, yes. My father was one of the most legendary lion tamers in the world. He taught me everything he knew.'

'Really?' said the ringmaster. 'Did he teach you how to make a lion jump through a flaming hoop?'

'Yes he did,' replied Lloyd.

'And did he teach you how to get six lions to form a pyramid?'

'Yes he did,' replied Lloyd.

'And have you ever stuck your head in a lion's mouth?'

'Just once,' replied Lloyd.

The ringmaster asked, 'Why only once?'

Lloyd said, 'I was looking for my father.'

First course
★ DISCOURSE ★

So, you're at a dinner hosted by your partner's parents. You've been briefed to avoid talking about politics, religion or Mum's disastrous hairdo. Here are a few other things not to say…

What exactly is this?

This is going to go right through me.

Oooh, someone's hungry.

Nice to see you can afford lobster now.

That looks… interesting…

This is nearly as good as my Mum makes it.

Do you know what they do to this before it's slaughtered?

This is lovely, but wouldn't it be better with _____?

'SOMETIMES YOU
JUST HAVE TO
BITE YOUR
UPPER LIP
AND PUT
SUNGLASSES ON.'

· BOB DYLAN ·

Legendary

★ PRANKS ★

Does the occasional practical joke help you become a
legend? Perhaps, but it is a risky strategy, so learn from
the master himself, George Clooney.
Here are some of his best...

The entertainment press was
getting excited about Brad Pitt and
Angelina Jolie's February wedding,
so George took advantage. He spread the word that the
wedding would take place at George's estate in Italy
where the weather was likely to be rainy and cold that
time of year. He ordered tables and a marquee for his
lawn and soon press helicopters were all over his estate
thinking the wedding was going to be there. It wasn't.

On the red carpet for the LA premiere of 'Hail, Caesar!', George persuaded Jonah Hill, Channing Tatum, Josh Brolin and Alden Ehrenreich that it would be a laugh for them all to all turn their backs on the press photographers. 'So we did it and George didn't,' said Alden. 'There's a great picture of George laughing at the camera with Josh and us looking like idiots.'

George found a gigantic, awful painting that someone had thrown away. He took it home, signed his name to it and framed it. When he was too busy to play golf with his friend Richard Evans, he would pretend to have art classes.

For Richard's 40th birthday, he said, 'This is the first painting my art teacher and I are both really proud of. You've been so supportive, I want you to have it.' Richard hung it over his couch for two years before he found out the true story.

Matt Damon was trying to lose weight for a role when he stayed at George's Italian home. George hired a tailor to take in Damon's clothes at the waist each day during his stay. 'He couldn't understand how he seemed to be gaining weight while he was trying so hard to lose it,' laughed George.

MAN OF MIRTH

Coming up

★ ROSES ★

A man called the emergency services and said, 'Good afternoon, I have just had my front garden landscaped, I have a nice new flower bed, a new fish pond with a fountain and a new rose garden.'

'That sounds lovely, sir,' said the operator, 'but I can't help you unless there is an emergency.'

'Well,' the man answered, 'the house next door is on fire and I don't want you to trample my front garden.'

MEET THE LEGEND
Simo
HÄYHÄ

Best known as: 'White Death' to the Soviet Army.

Did you know? When the Soviet Union invaded Finland in 1939, he donned white camouflage gear, grabbed his rifle and hid in a tree all day shooting enemy soldiers. At 20-40 degrees below zero. The Soviets sent out a whole task force to find Häyhä and take him out. He killed them all. Then they sent a team of counter-snipers. He killed all of them too. Then they carpet bombed the forest he was in. The shrapnel tore his coat.

Legendary fact: Over the course of 100 days, Häyhä took out 705 enemy combatants single-handed. He was finally stopped when a Russian shot him in the head with a banned explosive bullet. He survived and became a champion dog breeder after the war.

Quotable: When asked how he became such a good shooter, he answered: 'Practice'.

LEGEND OR LOSER?

★ **DIY** ★

Whether it's putting up a shelf, painting a bedroom or building a four-storey extension with helicopter pad, escape tunnel and death ray, there's always a niggling little job to occupy your weekend. So when it comes to home maintenance, do you have a screw loose or do you hit the nail on the head?

· THE PREPARATION ·

Legend: Clears the area, lays dust sheets, makes sure all tools and equipment are to hand before starting.

Loser: Opens a can of beer.

· THE TOOLS ·

Legend: A complete tool set at the ready, all tools regularly used, well cleaned and maintained.

Loser: Unused socket set, a bent screwdriver and 374 identical hex keys from Ikea. And the rusting electric drill borrowed from a neighbour who moved away seven years ago.

· THE HEIGHTS ·

Legend: A solid ladder with a friend or family member to steady it.

Loser: A swivel chair and a prayer.

· THE PRECAUTIONS ·

Legend: Uses an electronic tester to locate any hidden cabling or pipes.

Loser: Suddenly owns an indoor swimming pool. That is electrified.

· THE ENTERTAINMENT ·

Loser: Quiet radio for some background noise.

Loser: Plays favourite album at full volume. It's amazing where paint can travel when you use your brushes in the drum solo.

· THE END ·

Legend: Cleans all tools and puts them away. Tidies the area and runs the vacuum cleaner around.

Loser: Opens another beer in celebration. Wife tidies away the sharpest tools to give the kids a sporting chance of survival and calls in a local tradesman before the authorities condemn the house.

'I USED TO THINK ANYONE

DOING ANYTHING WEIRD WAS WEIRD.

NOW I KNOW THAT IT IS THE PEOPLE THAT CALL

OTHERS WEIRD THAT ARE WEIRD.'

· PAUL McCARTNEY ·

MEET THE LEGEND

Wolfgang Amadeus

MOZART

Best known as: One of the most gifted musicians in the history of classical music. A conductor, virtuoso pianist, organist and violinist, he wrote half the number of total symphonies he would create between the ages of 8 and 19.

Did you know? His full name was Johannes Chrysostomus Wolfgangus Theophilus Mozart. To save time, most of his friends called him Wolfie.

Legendary fact: Mozart was so skilled at playing the piano that for a party trick he would play it with the keys covered by a cloth.

Quotable: 'If I were obliged to marry all those with whom I have jested, I should have at least two hundred wives.'

TOP 5 TIPS
The
★ PARTY ★

Parties are a great place for mere mortals to witness your rise to legendary status. Here are a few ways you can stand out at the next barbecue, ball or birthday bash.

· WHEN TUNES MEET EARS ·

Be prepared with a few playlists that each have a well-sequenced blend of crowd-pleasers, current hits and a few forgotten favourites. Avoid the randomise button – it will reveal your secret Bieber obsession.

· WHEN HEAT MEETS BEER ·

Fill up a bucket, bath or basin with water and ice and pop your bottles in there. Contact with the cold water will chill the bottle faster than a freezer, where your bottle might explode and leave you with a lager and ice cream float.

· WHEN RED WINE MEETS CARPET ·

Blot it with a dry cloth or some paper towel to soak up the excess. Then use water and continue blotting it up rather than rubbing it deeper into the fibres. Pour white wine down your throat, not over a stain.

· WHEN BOOZE MEETS BRAIN ·

After a few drinks, always think twice before talking politics, posting anything on Instagram, chatting up the host, suggesting strip poker, or peeing anywhere but the toilet.

· WHEN HANGOVER MEETS EVERYTHING ·

Just before bed, drink a diarrhoea remedy available from your pharmacist. It will help with your low blood sugar and electrolyte imbalance. 'Hair of the dog' – morning booze – is just another punch to your already crying liver.

MAN OF MIRTH

Can you DIG IT?

A farmer was sent to jail. His wife was trying to hold the farm together until her husband was released. Unfortunately she was finding it very hard to keep up with all of the responsibilities of running a farm. She wrote a letter to him in jail: 'Dear sweetheart, I want to plant the potatoes. When is the best time to do it?'

Knowing that all the mail is checked by the prison authorities, the farmer wrote back: 'Honey, don't go near that field. That's where all the money is buried.'

As expected, the police arrived at the farm the following day and dug up the entire potato field to look for the money. After two full days of digging, they don't find anything.

The farmer then wrote to his wife: 'Honey, now is when you should plant the potatoes.'

'THERE WAS A KNOCK ON OUR DRESSING-ROOM DOOR. OUR MANAGER SHOUTED, 'KEITH! RON! **THE POLICE ARE HERE!**' OH, MAN, WE PANICKED, FLUSHED EVERYTHING DOWN THE JOHN. THEN THE DOOR OPENED AND IT WAS STEWART COPELAND AND STING.'

· KEITH RICHARDS ·

MEET THE LEGEND

Otto

ROHWEDDER

Best known as: The man who invented sliced bread, or at least the first commercial bread-slicing machine.

Did you know? He first had the idea in 1912 but it took until 1927 to build a working, reliable machine. One of the reasons it took so long was a fire in 1917 which destroyed his designs.

Legendary fact: He was a jeweller by trade, but was so convinced that the bread slicing machine would be a success that he sold his three jewellery stores to fund his efforts.

Quotable: The first sliced bread was advertised as 'The greatest forward step in the baking industry since bread was wrapped'.

'ANY IDIOT CAN
GET LAID WHEN
THEY'RE FAMOUS...
THAT'S EASY...
IT'S GETTING LAID
WHEN YOU'RE NOT
FAMOUS THAT TAKES
SOME TALENT.'

· KEVIN BACON ·

MAN OF MIRTH
Look before
YOU LEAP

Three drunkards were standing on top of the Empire State Building. The first one said to the other two, 'You know, it's a funny thing about these wind currents. Someone could jump off of this building right now and not even hit the ground; the updraft would carry them right back up to the top of the building.'

The second drunk said, 'You're crazy.'

The first drunk said, 'I'm serious. Watch!'

The first drunk jumped off of the building and moments later floated back up and landed awkwardly on the top.

The second drunk said, 'That's cool, let me try.'

So the second drunk leapt off of the building and promptly fell to the street below, splatting onto the pavement.

The first drunk smirked a little.

The third drunk looked at him and said, 'You know, Superman, you can be a real jerk when you're drunk.'

MEET THE LEGEND
Gabe
NEWELL

Best known as: Billionaire co-founder of Valve and the creator of the Steam PC gaming platform.

Did you know? He dropped out of Harvard to work for Microsoft where he had a key role in the first three releases of Windows. Gabe said that working at Microsoft was more of an education than his time at Harvard where he 'learned how to drink beer while doing a handstand in the snow'.

Legendary fact: Gabe has a private collection of over 600 knives.

Quotable: 'I want to be a giant space crab.'

LEGEND OR LOSER?

The
★ GYM ★

Even if you are not an occasional swimmer, captain of the football team, or training to be the first person to run to Mars, you still need to be fit and healthy. When you hit the gym are you a force for fitness or just another dumbbell?

· DRESS UP ·

Legend: Wears a clean top and shorts.
Good mid-range trainers.

Loser: Wears an old pair of shorts left over from school days that are now so tight they look like hot pants.

· DRESS UP ·

Legend: No noise beyond controlled breathing and the occasional note of exertion at the end of some hard reps.

Loser: Makes more grunts and groans than a hippo giving birth.

· TIE UP ·

Legend: Uses the machine for about 15-30 minutes depending on the exercise, then moves quickly on.

Loser: Puts towel on the machine 15 minutes before using it. Does two minutes of exercise to crack a sweat, then spends the next hour trying to get the perfect gym selfie.

· STEP UP ·

Legend: Happy to help spot someone while they bench press and ready to stop a novice from doing something clearly dangerous.

Loser: They have a calling as a personal trainer, even though this is their first ever visit to a gym.

· TIDY UP ·

Legend: Puts the dumbbells back on the rack after use. Always wipes down the machines.

Loser: Thinks Mum will pick up their weights after them. Is sure their sweat is a gift to others.

· CLEAN UP ·

Legend: Discreet in the changing room. Understands that all shapes and sizes will be there.

Loser: Comments loudly on everyone while blow-drying their tackle under the hand-dryer.

MAN OF MIRTH

Fishy

★ ★ TALES ★

An angling club was having its annual dinner and trophy presentation. A reporter from the local newspaper arrived to cover the event.

When the reporter entered the hall, they were surprised to see all the chairs spaced two metres apart. The reporter approached the caterer and said, 'That's a strange way to arrange seats for a party.'

The caterer replied, 'We always do it like that so that members can do full justice to their fish stories.'

'IF I HAD TO NAME MY
GREATEST STRENGTH,
I GUESS IT WOULD
BE MY HUMILITY.
GREATEST WEAKNESS,
IT'S POSSIBLE THAT
I'M A LITTLE TOO
AWESOME.'

· BARACK OBAMA ·

MEET THE LEGEND

Thomas

FITZPATRICK

Best known as: Pilot who landed a plane on a Manhattan road. Twice.

Did you know? At around 3am on September 30th, 1956, Fitzpatrick left a bar on St Nicholas Avenue, went to New Jersey and took a single-engine plane from the Teterboro School of Aeronautics. He took off without lights or radio contact and landed right back outside the bar. All because of a drunken bet.

Legendary fact: Two years later, drunk in a bar once more, someone didn't believe the story, so he did it all over again.

Quotable: To the police after the second flight, 'I didn't renew my pilot's license because I didn't want to fly again.'

MAN OF MIRTH

First

★ PUZZLE ★

The Vice President walked into the Oval Office and sees the President whooping and hollering.

'What's the matter, Mr. President?' the Vice President inquired.

'I just finished a jigsaw puzzle in record time!' the President beamed.

'How long did it take you?'

'Well, the box said '3 to 5 Years' but I did it in a month!'

MAN OF MIRTH

Two astronauts were in a spacecraft orbiting high above the earth. As part of the mission, one made a space walk while the other stayed inside.

When the space walk came to an end, the astronaut tried to get back inside the spacecraft. He discovered to his alarm that the cabin door was firmly locked.

So he knocked. There was no answer.

He knocked louder, much louder. There was still no answer.

Finally, he beat the door as hard as he could. Then he heard a voice from inside the spacecraft saying, 'Who's there?'

'IF YOU PLAY
A NICKELBACK
SONG BACKWARDS
YOU'LL HEAR
MESSAGES FROM
THE DEVIL.
EVEN WORSE, IF YOU
PLAY IT FORWARDS
YOU'LL HEAR
NICKELBACK.'

· DAVE GROHL ·

Criminally
★ STUPID ★

Some people become legendary through their mistakes.
We do not recommend this path.

Ashley Keast of
Rotherham, UK,
used a stolen
phone to snap a selfie
inside a house he was
burgling. He then
posted the picture
on WhatsApp, but
also sent the picture
to the victim's work
colleagues. He was jailed for two years and eight
months in 2014 after police found a stolen Rolex
watch, worth £4,000, hidden behind his radiator.

When Steven Fiorella, 19, presented 'his' driving licence at the Union Bar in Iowa City, USA, the doorman recognised it as his own licence, which had been reported stolen back in February.

A robbery victim was hysterical, showing officer Charanjit Meharu of the Calgary police the broken window and pointing out missing jewellery and electronics, when her French-speaking father called. Speaking in French, the victim explained that it was all a scam in order to get the insurance money. Unfortunately for the woman, Officer Meharu spoke six languages, including French.

Another smartphone/dumb criminal combo: Andrew Hennells boasted with a selfie on Facebook about his plans to raid a supermarket, including a picture of a knife and the words: 'Doing. Tesco. Over.' Police caught him 15 minutes later with the knife and £410 in stolen cash in King's Lynn, UK.

James Washington suffered a heart attack and confessed to a 17-year-old murder while approaching death... only to recover and get rewarded with life in prison for clearing his guilty conscience.

'I SEE MYSELF AS AN INTELLIGENT, SENSITIVE HUMAN, WITH THE SOUL OF A CLOWN WHICH FORCES ME TO BLOW IT AT THE MOST IMPORTANT MOMENTS.'

· JIM MORRISON ·

MEET THE LEGEND
Valentino
★ ROSSI ★

Best known as: One of the most successful MotoGP riders ever.

Did you know? Valentino is not shy at celebrating a win. Once he dressed up as Robin Hood and another time he took an inflatable Claudia Schiffer doll on a victory lap.

Legendary fact: Valentino's love of motorcycling doesn't stop at racing. He actively campaigns to keep it safe and has set up an academy to prepare the next generation of young riders for the rigours of the sport.

Quotable: 'My normal life is like being on holiday.'

MAN OF MIRTH

The price of

★ FAME ★

A famous actor walked into a bar and asked the barman if he could use the staff toilet.

'No,' said the barman, 'you can use the public one, just like everybody else!'

'Oh, come on man, you know who I am, please?' said the actor.

'No preferential treatment, either use the public toilet, or get out,' insisted the barman.

The actor considered his options for a moment while he hopped from foot to foot, before he gave in and went sheepishly into the men's room.

A few moments later he returned to the bar with his left trouser leg completely soaked.

'What the hell happened to you?!' exclaimed the barman.

'This happens every time,' said the actor, 'I go up to the urinal, and the guy standing next to me swings around saying 'Hey! You're famous!'

'I'M VERY GOOD AT DAYDREAMING. ASK ANY OF MY SCHOOLTEACHERS.'

· BRUCE DICKINSON ·

TOP 5 TIPS
Beating
★ THE ODDS ★

No one likes someone who wins every time, but a legend cannot lose every time either. Here are a few ideas to help tip the odds in your favour when losing is not an option.

· TOSSER ·

A coin toss is not a straight fifty-fifty. The odds are slightly more in favour of the coin landing facing the same way it was when tossed. If your opponent cannot catch and decides to spin the coin on a table the odds stray even further. The coin is more prone to land heavier side down – typically the head.

· CUTTER ·

f an inexperienced rock-paper-scissors player wins a
ound, there is a good chance they will stick with the
ame choice in the next round. Likewise, when they
ose, they are more prone to changing.

· BANKER ·

There are entire books on Monopoly strategy that
ake almost as long to read as it does to play a game.
Here are the best tips to remember – buy the orange
properties as they are the most visited on the board
and stop at three houses as they have the best return
on investment.

· STACKER ·

n Jenga, you can only use one hand at a time but that
doesn't mean you can't swap hands. Also, you can
balance the tower against your forearm, using your arm
as a brace. Is this cheating? No – this is the advice from
Leslie Scott, the person who wrote the rules.

· SKIPPER ·

f you want to be a champion stone skipper/skimmer,
first pick a flattish, triangular stone – circular stones
are less stable. Throw it out and down at the same
time, spinning it as hard as you can with a quick snap
of your wrist, aiming to hit the water parallel to
the surface.

'IT IS NICE TO BE RECOGNISED FOR ACTUALLY ACHIEVING SOMETHING IN LIFE AS OPPOSED TO SPENDING SEVEN WEEKS IN A HOUSE ON TV WITH A LOAD OF OTHER MUPPETS.'

· SIR BRADLEY WIGGINS ·

MAN OF MIRTH

Communication SKILLS

An old blacksmith realised he was getting a little long in the tooth for such strenuous work so he found a strong young man to become his apprentice.

The old fellow was crabby and everything had to be done his way without question. 'Keep your mouth shut and just do whatever I tell you to do,' he told the boy.

One day, the blacksmith took an iron out of the forge and laid it on the anvil. 'Get the hammer over there,' he said, 'and when I nod my head, hit it real good and hard.'

Now the town is looking for a new blacksmith.

MAN OF MIRTH

Beeping
DRIVER

One day Simon was driving with his 5-year-old daughter Lucy in the car and honked his car horn by mistake.

She immediately turned and looked at him with an expectant look on her face.

Seeing her look at him he said, 'I did that by accident.'

She replied, 'Oh, yes, I know that, daddy.'

He replied, 'How did you know?'

The girl said, 'Because you didn't say 'asshole' afterwards!'

'A GOOD FRIEND
WILL HELP
YOU MOVE, BUT
A TRUE FRIEND
WILL HELP
YOU MOVE
A BODY.'

· STEVEN J. DANIELS ·

LEGEND OR LOSER?

★ **FAN** ★

A great gig can be an
unforgettable experience.
But when you go to live music,
do you act like a superfan or
a superfool?

· LOGISTICS ·

Legend: Gets a good spot near-ish the front early on.
Ensures they are not blocking the view of anyone shorter.

Loser: When they hear the one song they know, they barge
straight to the front knocking everyone out of their way.

· LIQUID REFRESHMENT ·

Legend: Has a quick drink on the way to the gig and one
at the venue to avoid missing anything.

Loser: Completely tanked before leaving home, spends
the gig pushing past everyone getting more beers and/or
going to the toilet.

· PHOTOGRAPHY ·

Legend: Takes one quick photo to help remember a great gig.

Loser: Faces away from the stage to take fifteen selfies for each song. Films half the gig and insists on sharing the unedited video, even though the tinny music sounds like it's being played backwards through a sheep.

· CHORAL ABILITY ·

Legend: Sings along with a number of the songs.

Loser: Shouts misheard lyrics over the chorus.

· COMMUNICATION SKILLS ·

Loser: Understanding nod of artistic appreciation to their friends during a brilliant solo.

Loser: Talks the entire gig to anyone nearby about the sandwich they had for lunch, why their girlfriend left them, their journey, why their previous girlfriend left them, their last five holidays, why their previous-but-one girlfriend left them, why their boss sucks... All clues as to why their next girlfriend will leave them.

· EXITING THE VENUE ·

Legend: Chats about how great the gig was while politely joining the bustling queue to leave the building.

Loser: Charges senselessly to the door as if they miss their last train it will be a £40 taxi home. They fall asleep on the train, miss their stop and spend £80 on a taxi home.

'WHEN ARGUING
WITH A
STUPID PERSON,
BE SURE HE
ISN'T DOING THE
SAME THING.'

· ANONYMOUS ·

MEET THE LEGEND
Stephen
HAWKING

Best known as: Despite being diagnosed with amyotrophic lateral sclerosis (ALS) at 21, he became one of the greatest physicists of his generation.

Did you know? When he was 9 years old, his grades were among the worst in his class. Later in life he showed an interest in science by taking radios apart. However, he rarely put them back together again.

Legendary fact: He was born on January 8th, 1942 (300 years after the death of Galileo) and at 75 he was still determined to go into space.

Quotable: 'Someone told me that each equation I included in the book would halve the sales.'

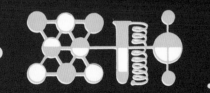

MAN OF MIRTH

Last

★ REQUESTS ★

Three prisoners were about to face a firing squad. In their last hours, they were asked what they would like to eat for their last meal.

The first prisoner asked for a juicy steak. He was served the steak and then taken away to be shot.

The second prisoner requested a burger. He was served the burger and then taken away to be shot.

The third prisoner asked for strawberries.

'Strawberries?' said the guard, 'But they're not in season.'

'That's fine,' said the prisoner, 'I'll wait.'

'WE ALL KNOW
THAT SMALL CARS ARE
GOOD FOR US. BUT SO
IS COD LIVER OIL.
AND JOGGING. I WANT
TO DRIVE AROUND IN
A TERMINATOR,
NOT THE HEROINE IN AN
E. M. FORSTER NOVEL.'

· JEREMY CLARKSON ·

MAN OF MIRTH

Relatively

LEGENDARY

Albert Einstein was touring universities across the United States, lecturing on his famous theories. He was always accompanied by his faithful chauffeur, Harry, who sat in the back row for every lecture.

After one lecture, Harry said, 'Professor Einstein,
I've heard your lecture on Relativity so many times that if
I had to, I could deliver it myself!'

'Very well,' replied Einstein, 'I'm going to Dartmouth next
week. They don't know me there. You can deliver the
lecture, and I'll take your place as chauffeur.'

So the following week in Dartmouth, Harry delivered
the lecture. He did not miss one word while Einstein sat in
the back row playing 'chauffeur' and enjoying a snooze
for a change.

However, just as Harry was concluding the lecture,
a research assistant interrupted him with a complex
question on the General Theory of Relativity.

Harry replied to the assistant, 'The answer to this question
is very simple! In fact, it's so simple that
I'm going to let my chauffeur answer it!'

'I OPENED THE DOOR FOR A LOT OF PEOPLE, AND THEY JUST RAN THROUGH AND LEFT ME HOLDING THE KNOB.'

· BO DIDDLEY ·

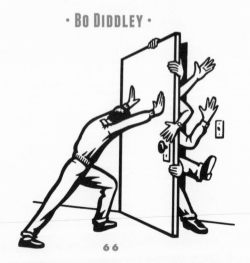

MAN OF MIRTH
Crazy, Crazy
KNIGHTS

One way or another, King Arthur is a legend. But let's not forget the other members of the Round Table:

Sir Cumflex - a knight with a strange accent

Sir Vey - the knight with a keen eye

Sir Cuitous - he approached his duties in a roundabout way

Sir Cumvent - the evasive knight

Sir Spicious - a paranoid knight

Sir Port - A great help to all the other knights

Sir Prise - who could always be relied on to do the unexpected

Sir Face - a handsome, but disappointingly shallow knight

Sir Real - adored melting clocks

Sir Cumference - the knight who designed the round table

Master of
★ SOME ★

A legend should not attempt to be a jack of all trades, but revealing a hidden talent does win serious legendary points. Here are a few well-known names with more than one string to their bow.

Christopher Walken once worked as a lion tamer.

Jimmy Stewart graduated near the top of his Architecture class at Princeton.

Not just able to fly the Millennium Falcon, Harrison Ford is a real pilot, once airlifting medical supplies to Haiti.

Johnny Cash trained as a military code breaker – he was one of the first Americans to hear the news of Stalin's death.

Film writer/director Mel Brooks deactivated enemy land mines during World War II.

Vanilla Ice, yes, Vanilla Ice, likes his extreme sports. He won three dirt biking championships and was once ranked the 6th best jet skier in the world.

Bond himself, Pierce Brosnan, is a skilled fire eater who has performed in the circus.

Justin Bieber, love him or loathe him, can do the Rubik's Cube in under 1 minute and 30 seconds.

Colin Farrell loves country line dancing and has even taught classes.

Rod Stewart has built an intricately detailed 1,500-square-foot model railway in his California home.

RoboCop, Peter Weller, holds a PhD in Art History.

Twilight star Taylor Lautner is a martial arts champion who received his black belt at the age of 8.

'FOR A
BRITISH PERSON
TO ENTER
BRITISH HEAVEN,
YOU BASICALLY
HAVE TO DIE
COMPLETELY
UNNOTICED
WITHOUT CAUSING
TOO MUCH OF A
KERFUFFLE.'

· JOHN OLIVER ·

MAN OF MIRTH

Last REQUESTS

A cowboy and a biker were sat on death row, due for execution on the same day. When the day arrived, the warden asked the cowboy if he had a last request.

'I sure do, warden,' replied the cowboy. 'I'd be mighty grateful if y'all play 'Achy Breaky Heart' for me before my time is up.'

'That's fine,' said the warden, 'we can do that. And you,' he said to the biker, 'do you have a last request?'

'Definitely,' said the biker. 'Kill me first.'

71

MEET THE LEGEND

Nikola

TESLA

Best known as: The inventor of many alternating current devices, including motors, generators and power distribution systems.

Did you know? Tesla knew that Mark Twain was suffering digestive problems and constipation so he invited him over to his lab. Tesla instructed Twain to stand on his 'earthquake machine' (an oscillating platform). After about 90 seconds, Twain jumped off the platform and bolted for the toilet.

Legendary fact: In 1901, Tesla described a new means of instant communication that involved gathering stock quotes and telegram messages, encoding the information and wirelessly broadcasting them to a device that would fit in your hand. Sound familiar?

Quotable: 'I don't care that they stole my idea... I care that they don't have any of their own.'

'HE HAS TURNED **DEFENSIVE BOXING** INTO A POETIC ART. TROUBLE IS, NOBODY EVER KNOCKED ANYBODY OUT WITH A POEM.'

· EDDIE SHAW, REFERRING
TO HEROL 'BOMBER' GRAHAM ·

TOP 5 TIPS

The

★ BARBECUE ★

If you only cook once a year, only outdoors and only over fire, and think it will be anywhere near edible, that makes you a typical man. A great barbecue takes more than guesswork. It takes a legend.

· SPINNING ·

Call it a kebab, call it a skewer – either way, call it tricky to turn on the barbecue without the food spinning and staying where it is when you try to turn it. How about using two off-centre skewers?

· DRYING ·

Dry your meat before cooking it on the grill. This stops wasting the energy required to evaporate the water. And the water prevents your meat browning on the outside. Flip it often for a quick, even cook that is less likely to become a burnt offering.

· SALTING ·

Do your homemade burgers fall apart on the grill? Adding salt to your ground beef when you make your burger dissolves some of the proteins and allows them to cross link. The health conscious may want to avoid too much salt, but as you're cooking red meat on an open flame, we guess you're not that bothered anyway.

· CLEANING ·

If you don't clean your grill after use, you leave a layer of grease behind. Next time you use it, it drips onto your flames, burns and you build up more grease. Which burns even more next time. This is not a layer of seasoned, browned yumminess but a charred, carcinogenic nightmare.

· TASTING ·

Guaiacol is an aroma compound produced when heat breaks down lignin, the resin that holds strands of cellulose together to form wood. It has a smoky, spicy, bacony aroma. Essentially, cooking over charcoal makes your food taste like bacon. BACON.

'ANY MAN WHO
CAN DRIVE SAFELY
WHILE KISSING
A PRETTY GIRL
IS SIMPLY NOT
GIVING THE KISS
THE ATTENTION IT
DESERVES.'

· ALBERT EINSTEIN ·

★ MEET THE LEGEND

Captain Jack

CHURCHILL

Best known as: 'Mad Jack' – the Scotsman who took a broadsword and longbow into battle. On the Normandy beaches during World War II.

Did you know? During a night raid on Nazi lines, his men captured 136 enemy soldiers, with Churchill himself capturing more than 40 Germans at sword point.

Legendary fact: Mad Jack fought until he was the last of his men standing during a battle on the island of Brac. Finally out of ammo, he stood his ground, playing his bagpipes until he was captured by the Germans and placed in a POW camp. From which he promptly escaped.

Quotable: 'On hearing that atomic bombs had been dropped on Japan: 'If it hadn't been for those damn Yanks, we could have kept the war going for another ten years!'

MAN OF MIRTH

Tongue

★ TIED ★

Even a legend will find these things
hard to say after five beers:

Ignominious

Pulchritudinous

Loquacious

Tergiversation

Trichotillomania

… and these will be completely
impossible to say after a few more:

I think I've had enough.

Sorry, but you're not really my type.

Seriously, no one wants to hear me sing.

That's right, I can't do a backflip.

Let's not steal this traffic cone.

'MOST FOOTBALL
PLAYERS ARE
TEMPERAMENTAL.
THAT'S 90
PERCENT TEMPER
AND 10 PERCENT
MENTAL.'

· DOUG PLANK ·

See me after
★ CLASS ★

The 'legends' of our school years tend to be remembered for one thing. Peeing off of the diving board, stealing the headmaster's wig or burning down the gym. And the physics lab. And half the county. However, such talents rarely transfer well into adult life. Thankfully, these school reports show that no matter how little promise you showed at Hopeless High, you can still turn things around.

· JOHN LENNON, MUSICIAN ·

'Certainly on the road to failure... hopeless... rather a clown in class... wasting other pupils' time.'

· STEPHEN FRY, COMEDIAN, ACTOR ·

'He has glaring faults and they have certainly glared at us this term.'

· GARY LINEKER, ENGLAND FOOTBALL CAPTAIN ·

'He must devote less of his time to sport if he wants to be a success. His academic work is handicapped by his excessive juvenility… too interested in sport. You can't make a living out of football.'

· WOODY ALLEN, COMEDIAN, DIRECTOR ·

'Suggested he seek counselling for his inability to take life seriously.'

· SIR RICHARD BRANSON, ENTREPRENEUR ·

'He will either go to prison or become a millionaire.'

· IAN FLEMING, CREATOR OF JAMES BOND ·

'Ought to make an excellent soldier, provided always that the ladies don't ruin him.'

· DAVID OWEN, POLITICIAN ·

'If I had to select an expedition to the South Pole he would be the first person I would choose. But I would make sure that he was not on the return journey.'

· NORMAN WISDOM, COMEDIAN ·

'The boy is every inch a fool, but luckily for him he's not very tall.'

· SIR WINSTON CHURCHILL ·

'He has no ambition. He is a constant trouble to everybody and is always in some scrape or other. He cannot be trusted to behave.'

· JEREMY PAXMAN, JOURNALIST ·

'Stubbornness is in his nature and could be an asset when directed to sound ends. But his flying off the handle will only mar his efforts and he must learn tact while not losing his outspokenness.'

'I WENT TO A FIGHT THE OTHER NIGHT, AND A HOCKEY GAME BROKE OUT.'

· RODNEY DANGERFIELD ·

MAN OF MIRTH

Felix Baumgartner was making a second record-breaking skydive attempt from a helium balloon in the stratosphere. Everything was going perfectly until in the closing metres of the skydive, he pulls the ripcord.

Nothing happens.

He tries again. Still nothing.

He starts to panic, but remembers his back-up chute. He pulls that cord.

Nothing happens.

He frantically begins pulling both cords, but to no avail. Suddenly, he looks down and he can't believe his eyes. Another man is in the air with him, but this guy appears to be going up. Just as they pass, Felix yells out, 'Hey, do you know anything about parachutes?'

The other guy yells back, 'No! Do you know anything about lighting gas ovens?'

MAN OF MIRTH

Getting the

★ SACK ★

My grandfather was a legend to me. He worked in a steel mill when he was a boy, and he used to tell me how he had toughened himself up so he could stand the rigours of the job.

He said he would stand outside behind the house and, with a 5-pound potato sack in each hand, extend his arms straight out to his sides and hold them there as long as he could.

After a while he tried 10-pound potato sacks, then 20-pound potato sacks and finally he got to where he could lift a 50-pound potato sack in each hand and hold his arms straight out for a five full minutes!

Eventually, he even started putting potatoes in the sacks.

MEET THE LEGEND

Miles

DAVIS

Best known as: Jazz trumpeter and band leader, who, by his own admission, 'changed the course of music five or six times'.

Did you know? On Miles' 13th birthday, his father bought him a new trumpet. This caused quite an argument in the Davis household as his mother wanted him to play the violin. Thankfully, as Miles once wrote, 'she soon got over it'.

Legendary fact: He had a very sharp tongue and often spoke his mind. One time bandmate John Coltrane was known for his beautiful, but lengthy, saxophone solos. When Coltrane explained that he couldn't find a way to stop, Davis quipped, 'You might try taking the horn out of your mouth'.

Quotable: 'You have to know 400 notes that you can play, then pick the right four.'

LEGEND OR LOSER?

Culinary

★ DELIGHTS ★

They say that the quickest way to someone's heart is through their stomach. 'They' have clearly not had any surgical training. But when you are in the kitchen, do you deserve a Michelin star or a wooden spoon?

· BREAKFAST ·

Legend: Happy to whip up their own hollandaise sauce to top an eggs florentine. And knows what eggs florentine is.

Loser: Toast.

· ELEVENSES ·

Legend: Can replicate their Gran's flapjack recipe at the drop of a hat. And will guard that recipe with their life.

Loser: Toast.

· LUNCH ·

Legend: Knows the secret to making a salad that actually looks worth eating.

Loser: Toast.

· EMERGENCIES ·

Legend: If there has been no chance to shop before some surprise guests arrive, will readily make a three-course meal with the 'fruits of the freezer'.

Loser: Toast.

· DINNER ·

Legend: Only had a ready meal once, and that was for a bet.

Loser: Toast.

· SUPPER ·

Legend: Can relieve the post-pub munchies with the perfect bacon, lettuce and tomato sandwich. All without setting fire to the kitchen.

Loser: Toast.

MAN OF MIRTH
A knight's
★ TALE ★

A knight returned with his men to his King's castle bearing many riches: bags of gold, fine jewels and several slave women.

'Where the hell have you been for the last week?' asked the King.

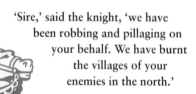

'Sire,' said the knight, 'we have been robbing and pillaging on your behalf. We have burnt the villages of your enemies in the north.'

'Wait,' said the King, 'I don't have any enemies in the north.'

'You do now, sire.'

MEET THE LEGEND

Tommy

FLOWERS

Best known as: Creating Colossus, the first programmable computer, at Bletchley Park during World War II to assist with code breaking.

Did you know? He was not one for 'turning it off and on again'. Tommy discovered that leaving the valves in his machines running all the time made them much more reliable.

Legendary fact: He built Colossus from scrounged telephone exchange equipment and parts he bought with his own money. He was awarded £1,000 for his war work, which did not cover his spending on Colossus.

Quotable: He described one of his own inventions as 'a Heath Robinson affair held together with string and sealing wax'.

Talk the
★ TALK ★

We enjoy watching our sporting heroes. They have
dedicated years of their life to reach the top. They
are living the dream. They are untouchable. They are
legends. Until they open their mouths...

· TERRY VENABLES ·

'If history is going to repeat itself, I should think we
can expect the same thing again.'

· RUUD GULLIT ·

'We must have had 99 per cent of the match. It was the
other three per cent that cost us.'

· CHARLES SHACKLEFORD ·

'I can dribble with my right hand and I can dribble
with my left hand. I'm amphibious.'

· GEORGE ROGERS ·

'I want to rush for 1,000 or 1,500 yards. Whichever comes first.'

· DENNIS RODMAN ·

'Chemistry is a class you take in high school or college, where you figure out two plus two is 10, or something.'

· JOE THEISMANN ·

'Nobody in football should be called a genius. A genius is a guy like Norman Einstein.'

· BRIAN KERR ·

'In his interviews, [David] Beckham manages to sit on the fence very well and keeps both ears on the ground.'

· KARL MALONE ·

'I ain't gonna be no escape-goat.'

MAN OF MIRTH
Wheelbarrow of
FORTUNE

An arrogant young man called Ryan started work at a building site. He started bragging that he could outdo anyone based on his superior strength. He was making fun of Jeff, one of the older workmen, in particular.

Eventually, Jeff had had enough. He said, 'Tell you what - why don't you put your money where your mouth is? I'll bet you a week's wages that I can take something over to that other building in this wheelbarrow and you won't be able to wheel it back.'

Ryan laughed confidently, 'You're on, old man. Let's see what you've got.'

So Jeff grabbed the wheelbarrow by the handles. Then he nodded to Ryan as he said with a smile, 'Alright. Get in.'

MEET THE LEGEND

PELÉ

Best known as: The greatest footballer of all time, according to many fans and players alike.

Did you know? In 1958, at age 17, Pelé simultaneously became the youngest player to participate, score, and win in a World Cup Final.

Legendary fact: On November 19th, 1969, Pelé scored his 1,000th career goal. Hundreds raced onto the pitch to celebrate with him and it took over 30 minutes for the game to resume. Santos still remember November 19th as 'Pelé Day'.

Quotable: 'Success isn't determined by how many times you win, but by how you play the week after you lose.'

MAN OF **MIRTH**

Out for the

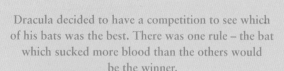

COUNT

Dracula decided to have a competition to see which
of his bats was the best. There was one rule – the bat
which sucked more blood than the others would
be the winner.

The first bat flew off and
came back after
10 minutes, its mouth
full of blood.

Dracula said,
'Congratulations, how
did you do it?'

The bat said, 'Do you see
that tower? Behind it to
the left there is a house.

I went in and sucked the
blood of all the family.'

'Well done,' said Dracula, 'very good.'

The second bat flew off and came back after 5
minutes, its face covered in blood.

Dracula was surprised at the speed, 'How did you
do that?'

The bat replied, 'Do you see that tower? Behind it to
the right there is a hotel. I went in and sucked the blood
of all the guests.'

'Well done,' said Dracula, 'fantastic!'

Finally, the third bat flew off and came back after just
1 minute, all of its body covered in blood.

Dracula doesn't believe his eyes, 'How did you do that?'

'Do you see that tower?' said the bat.

'Yes,' replied Dracula.

'I didn't.'

'WHO KNOWS THEIR
OWN STORY?
IT CERTAINLY
MAKES NO SENSE
WHEN YOU'RE IN
THE MIDDLE OF IT.'

· NICK CAVE ·